TOUGH
QUESTIONS
REVISED EDITION

DO SCIENCE AND THE BIBLE CONFLICT?

The Tough Questions Series

TOUGH QUESTIONS
REVISED EDITION

DO SCIENCE

AND THE

BIBLE

CONFLICT?

DO SCIENCE AND THE BIBLE CONFLICT?

JUDSON POLING
foreword by **Lee Strobel**

WILLOW
Willow Creek Resources

ZONDERVAN™

GRAND RAPIDS, MICHIGAN 49530 USA

We want to hear from you. Please send your comments about this book to us in care of zreview@zondervan.com. Thank you.

ZONDERVAN™

Do Science and the Bible Conflict?
Copyright © 1998, 2003 by Willow Creek Association

Requests for information should be addressed to:

Zondervan, *Grand Rapids, Michigan 49530*

ISBN: 0-310-24507-9

Interior design by Nancy Wilson

Printed in the United States of America

08 09 10 /❖ CH/ 10 9 8 7

Contents

Foreword

For most of my life I was an atheist. I thought that the Bible was hopelessly riddled with mythology, that God was a man-made creation born of wishful thinking, and that the deity of Jesus was merely a product of legendary development. My no-nonsense education in journalism and law contributed to my skeptical viewpoint. In fact, just the idea of an all-powerful, all-loving, all-knowing creator of the universe seemed too absurd to even justify the time to investigate whether there could be any evidence backing it up.

However, my agnostic wife's conversion to Christianity, and the subsequent transformation of her character and values, prompted me to launch my own spiritual journey in 1980. Using the skills I developed as the legal affairs editor of *The Chicago Tribune,* I began to check out whether any concrete facts, historical data, or convincing logic supported the Christian faith. Looking back, I wish I had this curriculum to supplement my efforts.

This excellent material can help you in two ways. If you're already a Christ-follower, this series can provide answers to some of the tough questions your seeker friends are asking—or you're asking yourself. If you're not yet following Christ but consider yourself either an open-minded skeptic or a spiritual seeker, this series can also help you in your journey. You can thoroughly and responsibly explore the relevant issues while discussing the topics in community with others. In short, it's a tremendous guide for people who really want to discover the truth about God and this fascinating and challenging Nazarene carpenter named Jesus.

If the previous paragraph describes you in some way, prepare for the adventure of a lifetime. Let the pages that follow take you on a stimulating journey of discovery as you grapple with the most profound—and potentially life-changing—questions in the world.

—Lee Strobel, author of
The Case for Christ and *The Case for Faith*

Getting Started

Welcome to the Tough Questions series! This small group curriculum was produced with the conviction that claims regarding spiritual truth can and should be tested. Religions—sometimes considered exempt from scrutiny—are not free to make sweeping declarations and demands without providing solid reasons why they should be taken seriously. These teachings, including those from the Bible in particular, purport to explain the most significant of life's mysteries, with consequences alleged to be eternal. Such grand claims should be analyzed carefully. If this questioning process exposes faulty assertions, it only makes sense to refuse to place one's trust in these flawed systems of belief. If, on the other hand, an intense investigation leads to the discovery of truth, the search will have been worth it all.

Christianity contends that God welcomes sincere examination and inquiry; in fact, it's a matter of historical record that Jesus encouraged such scrutiny. The Bible is not a secret kept only for the initiated few, but an open book available for study and debate. The central teachings of Christianity are freely offered to all, to the skeptic as well as to the believer.

So here's an open invitation: explore the options, examine the claims, and draw your conclusions. And once you encounter and embrace the truth—look out! Meaningful life-change and growth will be yours to enjoy.

It is possible for any of us to believe error; it is also feasible for us to resist truth. Using this set of discussion guides will help you sort out the true from the supposed, and ultimately offer a reasonable defense of

> You will seek me and find me when you seek me with all your heart.
>
> —Jeremiah 29:13

the Christian faith. Whether you are a nonbeliever or skeptic, or someone who is already convinced and looking to fortify your faith, these guides will lead you to a fascinating exploration of vital spiritual truths.

Tough Questions for Small Groups

The Tough Questions series is specifically designed to give spiritual seekers (or non-Christians) a chance to raise questions and investigate the basics of the Christian faith within the safe context of a seeker small group. These groups typically consist of a community of two to twelve seekers and one or two leaders who gather on a regular basis, primarily to discuss spiritual matters. Seeker groups meet at a wide variety of locations, from homes and offices to restaurants and churches to bookstores and park district picnic tables. A trained Christian leader normally organizes the group and facilitates the discussions based on the seekers' spiritual concerns and interests. Usually, at least one apprentice (or coleader) who is also a Christian assists the group leader. The rest of the participants are mostly, if not all, non-Christians. This curriculum is intended to enhance these seeker small group discussions and create a fresh approach to exploring the Christian faith.

Because the primary audience is the not-yet-convinced seeker, these guides are designed to represent the skeptical, along with the Christian, perspective. While the truths of the Christian position are strongly affirmed, it is anticipated that non-Christians will dive into these materials with a group of friends and discover that their questions and doubts are not only well understood and represented here, but also valued. If that goal is accomplished, open and honest discussions about Christianity can follow. The greatest hope behind the formation of this series is that seekers will be challenged in a respectful way to seriously consider and even accept the claims of Christ.

A secondary purpose behind the design of this series is to provide a tool for small groups of Christians to use as they discuss answers to the tough questions seekers are asking. The process of wrestling through these important questions and issues will not only strengthen their own personal faith but also provide them with insights for entering into informed dialogues about Christianity with their seeking friends.

A hybrid of the two options mentioned above may make more sense for some groups. For example, a small group of Christians may want to open up their discussion to include those who are just beginning to investigate spiritual things. This third approach provides an excellent opportunity for both Christians and seekers to examine the claims of Christianity together. Whatever the configuration of your group, may you benefit greatly as you use these guides to fully engage in lively discussions about issues that matter most.

Guide Features

The Introduction

At the beginning of every session is an introduction, usually several paragraphs long. You may want to read this beforehand even thought your leader will probably ask the group to read it aloud together at the start of every meeting. These introductions are written from a skeptical point of view, so a full spectrum of perspectives is represented in each session. Hopefully, this information will help you feel represented, understood, and valued.

Open for Discussion

Most sessions contain ten to fifteen questions your group can discuss. You may find that it is difficult for your group to get through all these questions in one sitting. That is okay; the important thing is to engage in the topic at hand—not to necessarily get through every question. Your group, however, may decide to spend more than one meeting on each session in order to address all of the questions. The Open for Discussion sections are designed to draw out group participation and give everyone the opportunity to process things openly.

Usually, the first question of each session is an "icebreaker." These simple questions are designed to get the conversation going by prompting the group to discuss a nonthreatening issue, usually having to do with the session topic to be covered. Your group may want to make time for additional icebreakers at the beginning of each discussion.

Heart of the Matter

The section called "Heart of the Matter" represents a slight turn in the group discussion. Generally speaking, the questions in this section speak more to the emotional, rather than just the intellectual, side of the issue. This is an opportunity to get in touch with how you feel about a certain aspect of the topic being discussed and to share those feelings with the rest of the group.

Charting Your Journey

The purpose of the "Charting Your Journey" section is to challenge you to go beyond a mere intellectual and emotional discussion to personal application. This group experience is, after all, a journey, so each session includes this section devoted to helping you identify and talk about your current position. Your views will most likely fluctuate as you make new discoveries along the way.

Straight Talk

Every session has at least one section, called "Straight Talk," designed to stimulate further thinking and discussion around relevant supplementary information. The question immediately following Straight Talk usually refers to the material just presented, so it is important that you read and understand this part before you attempt to answer the question.

Quotes

Scattered throughout every session are various quotes, many of them from skeptical or critical points of view. These are simply intended to spark your thinking about the issue at hand.

Recommended Resources

This section at the back of each guide lists recommended books that may serve as helpful resources for further study.

Discussion Guidelines

These guides, which consist mainly of questions to be answered in your group setting, are designed to elicit dialogue rather than short, simple answers. Strictly speaking, these guides are not Bible studies, though they regularly refer to biblical themes and passages. Instead, they are topical discussion guides, meant to get you talking about what you really think and feel. The sessions have a point and attempt to lead to some resolution, but they fall short of providing the last word on any of the questions raised. That is left for you to discover for yourself! You will be invited to bring your experience, perspective, and uncertainties to the discussion, and you will also be encouraged to compare your beliefs with what the Bible teaches in order to determine where you stand as each meeting unfolds.

Your group should have a discussion leader. This facilitator can get needed background material for each session in the *Tough Questions Leader's Guide*.

There, your leader will find some brief points of clarification and understanding (along with suggested answers) for many of the questions in each session. The supplemental book *Seeker Small Groups* is also strongly recommended as a helpful resource for leaders to effectively start up small groups and facilitate discussions for spiritual seekers. *The Complete Book of Questions: 1001 Conversation Starters for Any Occasion,* a resource filled with icebreaker questions, may be a useful tool to assist everyone in your group to get to know one another better, and to more easily launch your interactions.

In addition, keep the following list of suggestions in mind as you prepare to participate in your group discussions.

1. The Tough Questions series does not necessarily need to be discussed sequentially. The guides, as well as individual sessions, can be mixed and matched in any order and easily discussed independently of each other, based on everyone's interests and questions.

2. If possible, read over the material before each meeting. Familiarity with the topic will greatly enrich the time you spend in the group discussion.

3. Be willing to join in the group interaction. The leader of the group will not present a lecture but rather will encourage each of you to openly discuss your opinions and disagreements. Plan to share your ideas honestly and forthrightly.

4. Be sensitive to the other members of your group. Listen attentively when they speak and be affirming whenever you can. This will encourage more hesitant members of the group to participate. Always remember to show respect toward the others even if they don't always agree with your position.

5. Be careful not to dominate the discussion. By all means participate, but allow others to have equal time.
6. Try to stick to the topic being studied. There won't be enough time to handle the peripheral tough questions that come to mind during your meeting.
7. It would be helpful for you to have a good modern translation of the Bible, such as the New International Version, the New Living Translation, or the New American Standard Bible. You might prefer to use a Bible that includes notes especially for seekers, such as *The Journey: The Study Bible for Spiritual Seekers.* Unless noted otherwise, questions in this series are based on the New International Version.
8. Do some extra reading in the Bible and other recommended books as you work through these sessions. The "Recommended Resources" section at the back of each guide offers some ideas of books to read.

Unspeakable Love

Christianity stands or falls on Christ. Yet he left us with a whole lot of hard sayings. But the central scandal of Christianity is that at a point in history, God came down to live among us in a person, Jesus of Nazareth. And the most baffling moment of Jesus' life was on the cross, where he hung to die like a common criminal. In that place of weakness—where all seemed lost, where the taunts of "Prove yourself, Jesus, and come down from there!" lashed out like the whip that flogged him prior to his crucifixion—somehow God was at his best. There at the cross, he expressed a love greater than words could ever describe. That act of Jesus, presented as the ultimate demonstration of the love and justice of God, begs to be put to "cross" examination.

As you wrestle with these tough questions, be assured that satisfying, reasonable answers are waiting to be found. And you're invited to discover them with others in your small group as you explore and discuss these guides. God bless you on your spiritual journey!

Seek and you will find; knock and the door will be opened to you.

—Matthew 7: 7

Do Science and the Bible Conflict?

Stop any person on the street and ask his or her opinion of modern science. "Fantastic! Amazing! What a time to be alive!" Modern science has touched all our lives for the better. Ask the same individual about his or her views on modern religion, and you'll probably get a less enthusiastic response. "Boring. Irrelevant. Waste of time." Few people seem to be able to get as excited about religion—and many are outwardly antagonistic. Perhaps Carl Sagan best illustrated these attitudes when he said, "If you want to save your child from polio, you can pray or you can inoculate. . . . Try science" (quoted in *2000 Years of Disbelief, Famous People with the Courage to Doubt* by James A. Haught).

For many people, science has sounded the death knell for God. It has shown that God probably doesn't exist, because all the things we previously used God to explain can now be understood as produced by natural processes rather than an all-powerful deity. Even if God does exist, he's irrelevant—a bystander in the cosmic drama that began with a Big Bang, became more complex, and eventually achieved consciousness by means of undirected evolution. This drama has now culminated in a part of the universe—humanity—looking back on itself and learning where it came from.

Contempt for religion is not just a product of modern science. Generations ago Thomas Paine wrote,

"The study of theology, as it stands in the Christian churches, is the study of nothing; it is founded on nothing; it rests on no principles; it proceeds by no authority; it has no data; it can demonstrate nothing; and it admits of no conclusion." More recently American rationalist Paul Keller wrote, "Faith is a euphemism for prejudice and religion is a euphemism for superstition." With guns like these aimed at religion, how can it hope to stand, unless people simply close their eyes to the overwhelming evidence from science and retreat back into ignorance and fear reminiscent of the Dark Ages?

Has science made religion obsolete? Is the Bible a vestige from an era when people were uncritical and would accept anything without proof? Why shouldn't we throw out the Bible in favor of the more reliable truths of science? This guide will help you explore these tough questions.

Isn't Christianity Based on Blind Faith?

Faith Like a Child

A little boy raises his hand in Sunday school. "Teacher, how do we know there's a God?" The teacher smiles and answers, "You can't know; you just have to believe in him by faith." A little girl raises her hand. "What's faith?" The boy blurts out, "Oh, I know the answer to that one. Faith means believing something you know isn't true."

Is that what faith is: belief that flies in the face of evidence? Maybe that's too harsh. Maybe by faith people mean believing even when you don't have evidence. This definition seems to fit a lot of people who claim to be Christians. Christianity is, after all, a "faith," so it must mean that the followers of Christianity are people of faith. But too many Christians remind us of the person who was heard to exclaim, "My mind's made up; don't confuse me with the facts!" They are people commended for belief and rebuked for doubt. The Bible isn't to be picked apart; it's meant to be read and believed. Isn't a child held up as an example of how to have faith? What child resorts to a detailed, scientific analysis of anything?

It is often pointed out that the Bible is prescientific. Jesus and the apostle Paul were certainly not scientists. And many of the followers of Christianity have argued for decidedly unscientific views: the earth as the center of the solar system, the sky as a hard shell covering the

> So far as I can remember, there is not one word in the Gospels in praise of intelligence.
>
> —Bertrand Russell

earth, a view of disease that says demons rather than germs cause sickness, to name just a few. Throughout history, science has been tolerated by the church only as long as it hasn't contradicted matters of faith. And when it has contradicted faith, science has been asked to bow politely and leave the room.

It seems fair, in light of history and experience, to propose that religion—and Christianity in particular—is based not on experimentation and analysis but on faith. You either believe or you don't, and what ultimately convinces you will be some sort of experience (imagined or otherwise) or visitation by God (or possibly nothing but your earnest desire to believe) rather than study and research. Robert Heinlein, the prolific science fiction writer, observed in *Notebooks of Lazarus Long,* "History does not record anywhere at any time a religion that has any rational basis. Religion is a crutch for people not strong enough to stand up to the unknown without help. But, like dandruff, most people do have a religion and spend time and money on it and seem to derive considerable pleasure from fiddling with it." If that's truly the case, no wonder science and religion have not gotten along well.

It is also true that it is futile to try to convince someone of spiritual dogma by using reason when the essence of it is not something reasonable (for example, belief in an unseen God who can't be known through material means). The skeptic predicts it *won't* work, and the true believer says it *shouldn't* work.

So what's the point of a reasoned approach to Christianity, when the whole system is based on faith?

It vexes me when they would constrain science by the authority of the Scriptures, and yet do not consider themselves bound to answer reason and experiment.

—Galileo Galilei,
The Authority of Scripture in Philosophical Controversies

Invisible Pink Unicorns are beings of awesome mystical power. We know this because they manage to be invisible and pink at the same time. Like all religions, the Faith of the Invisible Pink Unicorns is based upon both logic and faith. We have faith that they are pink; we logically know that they are invisible because we can't see them.

—Steve Eley

1. On the continuum below, mark the spot that best indicates how you were brought up to believe in spiritual things.

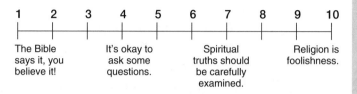

1	2	3	4	5	6	7	8	9	10

The Bible says it, you believe it!   It's okay to ask some questions.   Spiritual truths should be carefully examined.   Religion is foolishness.

2. On the continuum below, mark the spot that best indicates how you were brought up to believe in science.

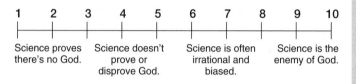

1	2	3	4	5	6	7	8	9	10

Science proves there's no God.   Science doesn't prove or disprove God.   Science is often irrational and biased.   Science is the enemy of God.

3. Which of the following definitions of faith can you most relate to? Explain.

- Faith means believing something you know is not true.
- Faith is a "great excuse to evade the need to think and evaluate evidence."
- Faith is "based on a deep-seated need to believe."
- Faith is simply filling in the gaps when you have probability but not certainty.

4. Mark the following statements true or false, according to your current way of thinking. Give reasons for your answers.

_____ Faith is required to believe in God, because there is no evidence for his existence.

_____ If you have reasons for something, you don't need faith; if you have faith, reasons don't matter.

_____ It is foolish to believe something just because a spiritual authority says so.

_____ There are plenty of reasons to believe in Christianity; faith is just quicker and easier than reason.

_____ God prefers that people believe in him by faith, but will give reasons if he has to.

5. Christianity is called a faith; it is not called a science. Does this matter to you? Why or why not? What would need to change for it to be called a science?

6. In your opinion, is Christianity based on fact or on faith? Explain your answer.

7. How certain are you that your current perspective on the truth (or unreliability) of Christianity is correct? What would lead you to greater certainty about your current position? What would lead you to serious doubt about it?

8. What do you think of the statement "Christianity sometimes goes beyond reason but not against it"?

STRAIGHT TALK

Blind Faith?

While it is true that faith is a part of Christianity, the Bible nowhere commands — or commends — putting faith in faith. Christians are instructed to put their faith in facts and ultimately put their trust in a person, Jesus Christ. Blind obedience to any message without examining its reliability is not biblical Christianity — it is a great way to get sucked into a cult! The Bible commands people to investigate, not to put faith in everything that comes along. People should put trust only in worthy recipients. This is why idolatry is so forcefully condemned — not because God has an ego problem but because any "god" other than he will prove unreliable.

Peter, one of Jesus' closest disciples, did not appeal to his readers to blindly accept his message. He made it clear that there were objective facts which were reliable, and that there were also fairy tales to be avoided. "We did not follow cleverly invented stories when we told you about the power and coming of our Lord Jesus Christ, but we were eyewitnesses of his majesty" (2 Peter 1:16). The people of Berea were commended because when the apostle Paul preached in their city, they made sure his message had validity: "The Bereans were of more noble character than the Thessalonians, for they received the message with great eagerness and examined the Scriptures every day to see if what Paul said was true" (Acts 17:11). Such examples make it clear that faith is not credulity, and careful investigation and inquiry ought to be normal operating procedure in the spiritual realm as well as elsewhere.

9. What do you think is the role of reason in the life of a Christian? What are the limits of our powers of reasoning?

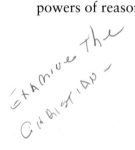

Examine The
Christian

10. Why do you think some people become angry when they are asked to put faith or trust in God?

FAITH IN WEAKNESS

11. Why do you think some people get angry when they are asked to give clear reasons for what they believe?

> Reality is that which, when you stop believing in it, doesn't go away.
>
> —Philip K. Dick

12. Do you think anyone is capable of living without some kind of faith in something? Why or why not?

CHARTING YOUR JOURNEY

With this session you're beginning a journey. Keep in mind that you do not need to feel pressured to "say the right thing" at any point during these discussions. You're taking the time to do this work because you want answers and because you're willing to be honest with your doubts and uncertainties. You may also have others in your life who would benefit from hearing about what you'll be learning. So use these sessions profitably—ask the tough questions, think "outside the box," learn from what others in your group have to say. But keep being authentic about where you are in your process.

To help you see yourself more clearly, throughout this guide you will have an opportunity to indicate where you are in your spiritual journey. As you gain more information, you may find yourself reconsidering your opinions from session to session. The important thing is for you to be completely truthful about what you believe—or don't believe—right now.

13. On a scale from one to ten, place an *X* near the spot and phrase that best describes you. What reasons do you have for placing your *X* where you did?

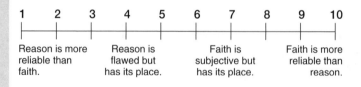

Why Are So Few Scientists Christians?

Minds at War

Most people do not view intelligent scientists as devoted believers in God. There's something in our psyche which imagines that the skeptical, questioning scientist does not fit with the faith-filled, anti-intellectual religious person. The scientist takes nothing for granted; the religious person believes what he's told to believe. The scientist needs evidence; the religious person exercises faith. The scientist wants to explain; the religious person defers to "mystery." The two fields seem not only widely separated but at odds with each other.

History bears witness to this animosity. We all remember the story of how the church opposed Galileo when he proposed that the earth went around the sun. Elizabeth Cady Stanton expressed the obvious narrowness of religion when she wrote in *The Woman's Bible,* "All through the centuries scholars and scientists have been imprisoned, tortured and burned alive for some discovery which seemed to conflict with a petty text of Scripture. Surely the immutable laws of the universe can teach more impressive and exalted lessons than the holy books of all the religions on earth." In 1925 H. L. Menken wrote, "Religion is fundamentally opposed to everything I hold in veneration—courage, clear thinking, honesty, fairness, and above all, love of the truth." Even recently, when the Vatican—having

> The church says the earth is flat, but I know that it is round, for I have seen the shadow on the moon, and I have more faith in a shadow than in the church.
>
> —Ferdinand Magellan

learned an important lesson about tolerance from history—invited scientists to advise it on cosmology, the pope personally told the scientists not to inquire into the Big Bang, because that was the moment of Creation and therefore the work of God. What scientist would submit to such a request? Why would the pope think it improper to research any area of knowledge, since he believes that the whole universe, not just the Big Bang, is God's work? Clearly, these two groups have radically different agendas, and both seem to think the other is stepping out of bounds.

So it's not surprising that the majority of scientists aren't members of any religion. According to *Newsweek* (June 29, 1987), "By one count there are some 700 scientists with respectable academic credentials (out of a total of 480,000 U.S. earth and life scientists, less than 0.2%) who give credence to creation-science, the general theory that complex life forms did not evolve but appeared 'abruptly.'" Yet if Christian truth is truth, why don't our greatest minds accept these truths as well as truths of nature and observation? Why wouldn't the knowledge of God be the easiest for a brilliant mind to grasp—unless spiritual truths don't make logical sense and appeal only to the simpleminded?

This session will explore the tension between men and women of faith and men and women of science. You can judge for yourself if the lack of religious belief among scientists is evidence that religious belief lacks credibility, or if some other explanation fits better.

1. Check the statements below that best fit the beliefs of your growing-up years. Explain what factors shaped your opinions.

_____ Scientists have invented bombs, radioactive waste, environmental hazards, and other terrible creations without caring about the effects of their work.

_____ Scientists have too much power and influence over how the world is progressing.

_____ Scientists are geeks who have great minds but poor social and personal skills.

_____ Scientists are brilliant members of society and should be consulted whenever we need advice about a problem.

_____ Scientists are among the few people left in society who never let personal bias color their thinking or conclusions.

_____ Scientists are the hope of our future; they are great role models.

> The world holds two classes of men—intelligent men without religion, and religious men without intelligence.
>
> —Abu'l-Ala-Al-Ma'arri, Syrian poet (A.D. 973–1057)

2. When you were growing up, did people you knew who were scientifically inclined tend to be skeptical about spiritual matters? How about people who were spiritually minded—

did they tend to be scientifically ignorant? What effect did these experiences have on the formation of your views of science and religion?

3. Some people think science flows from facts (without any faith) and religion flows from faith (without any facts). What do you think of that distinction?

4. Some people think that the only way to be a Christian and a scientist at the same time is to set aside Christian beliefs so they don't color the outcome of research. What do you think of this approach? If you were a scientist, what would be your approach in trying to be objective while also believing in Jesus and the Bible?

5. It is often claimed that scientists are extremely objective. Do you think this is always true? What factors besides pure facts could affect a scientist's opinions?

After becoming disillusioned with the research and work on super string theory because speculations were so far beyond any possible empirical test, Sheldon Glashow (physicist and Nobel Prize recipient) remarked: "For the first time since the Dark Ages, we can see how our noble [scientific] search may end, with faith replacing science once again."

—quoted by John Horgan in *The End of Science*

6. Consider the following quote by Richard Dawkins.

It is often said, mainly by the "no-contests," that although there is no positive evidence for the existence of God, nor is there evidence against his existence. So it is best to keep an open mind and be agnostic. At first sight that seems an unassailable position, at least in the weak sense of Pascal's wager. But on second thought it seems a cop-out, because the same could be said of Father Christmas and tooth fairies. There may be fairies at the bottom of the garden. There is no evidence for it, but you can't prove that there aren't any, so shouldn't we be agnostic with respect to fairies?

What do you think is the difference between being open to the possibility of a God and being open to the possible existence of fairies?

STRAIGHT TALK

The Bias of Science

A person who believes in God recognizes there are natural events, like a tornado, as well as supernatural events (miracles), like the resurrection of Jesus. Reality, to a theist, comprises both spheres. Modern science, however, recognizes only natural events and explanations. Before any data have been collected, those who use a naturalistic methodology exclude God.

What happens when science looks at so-called supernatural events? What is clear is what will *never* happen: the scientific method will never allow for the involvement of a transcendent God. The only explanations that will be acceptable omit references to God even if the data seem to point to divine involvement.

Phillip Johnson points out the problem of refusing to acknowledge this bias, when he says, "Methodological naturalism — the principle that science can study only the things that are accessible to its instruments and techniques — is not in question. Of course science can study only what science can study . . . That science has its limitations is not in doubt; the question is whether unsound assumptions about reality have been made to permit science to escape those limitations."

Science's bias against the supernatural comes from someplace other than science, because the scientific method has that bias prior to any investigation of phenomena. It sounds scientific to say, "I will only allow for naturalistic explanations in my research," but it is actually a philosophic and unscientific statement about the nature of reality in the name of science.

7. Do you agree with the above Straight Talk that the decision to rule out God as a possible explanation for a phenomenon is based not on science but on "unsound assumptions about reality"? Explain.

8. A zoologist named D. M. S. Watson once wrote, "Evolution has been accepted by scientists, not because it has been observed to occur or proved by logical coherent evidence to be true, but because the only alternative, special creation, is clearly unacceptable." Do you think it's rational to rule out, before considering the evidence, the possible involvement of God in creating the universe? Why or why not?

9. If I carry a book across the room and then say, "Explain how the book got here," but tell you that human agency is not an option, am I being scientific? How is this example similar to or unlike ruling out God when trying to explain creation or historical events such as the resurrection of Jesus?

10. One definition of *scientism* says that "science is the very paradigm of truth and rationality. . . . everything outside of science is a matter of mere belief and subjective opinion. . . . science, exclusively and ideally, is our model of intellectual excellence" (J. P. Moreland, *The Creation Hypothesis*). Does scientism contain any emotional or faith elements? How is scientism different from the pure practice of science?

11. Do you find yourself being stirred emotionally as you discuss the objectivity—or lack thereof—within the scientific community? If so, what's at the heart of your emotional response? If not, what do you think provokes people who do feel a reaction?

12. Some of the greatest minds of science have also been believers in God (Newton, Galileo, Kepler, Boyle, Faraday, Pasteur, Joule, and Jastrow, to name a few). What do you think explains the current prevailing attitude that brilliant thinkers couldn't possibly have objective reasons for their views about God?

13. Centuries before Copernicus, the prevailing scientific view was that the earth was the center of the solar system. The church adopted that idea and tried to find biblical support. When science changed, the church looked foolish for "biblicizing" an outdated scientific position. What lesson could modern believers learn from this historical example?

For the scientist who has lived by his faith in the power of reason, the story ends like a bad dream. He has scaled the mountains of ignorance; he is about to conquer the highest peak; as he pulls himself over the final rock, he is greeted by a band of theologians who have been sitting there for centuries.

—Robert Jastrow,
God and the Astronomer

14. On a scale from one to ten, place an X near the spot and phrase that best describes your view. What reasons do you have for placing your X where you did?

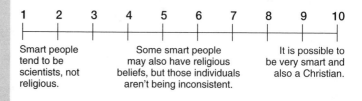

1 2 3 4 5 6 7 8 9 10

Smart people tend to be scientists, not religious.

Some smart people may also have religious beliefs, but those individuals aren't being inconsistent.

It is possible to be very smart and also a Christian.

Doesn't the Big Bang Disprove a Creator?

A Noisy Beginning

In 1965 two scientists were testing their ultrasensitive microwave radiation detector. The machine was apparently malfunctioning, because no matter where they pointed it, it was picking up a low-grade "hum" of microwaves. They discovered bird droppings on the detector, but even after cleaning it, the noise persisted. This continued for months; no matter which way it was aimed, there was a three-degree Kelvin radiation coming from every direction in the universe.

What these scientists discovered was the "echo" of the Big Bang. These findings were confirmed and refined by a satellite called COBE (Cosmic Background Explorer). When the COBE found slight ripples in the radiation in 1992—exactly what was predicted as necessary to explain the formation of galaxies—Stephen Hawking, the brilliant Cambridge professor and cosmologist, called it "the discovery of the century, if not of all time."

The significance of the Big Bang has been argued, though it is widely accepted as fact. When Carl Sagan wrote his introduction to Hawking's best-seller *A Brief History of Time,* he noted, "Hawking is attempting, as he explicitly states, to understand the mind of God. And this makes all the more unexpected the conclusion of the effort, at least so far: a universe with no edge in space, no beginning or end in time, and nothing for a

Creator to do." A year after his book was released, Hawking wrote elsewhere, "What I have done is to show that it is possible for the way the universe began to be determined by the laws of science. In that case, it would not be necessary to appeal to God to decide how the universe began. This doesn't prove that there is no God, only that God is not necessary."

If we believe there is no God, our understanding of the universe and our place in it will be drastically different from that of someone who believes there is a personal deity who created us. As Richard Dawkins wrote in *River Out of Eden: A Darwinian View of Life*, "If the universe were just electrons and selfish genes, meaningless tragedies like the crashing of this bus [full of schoolchildren] are exactly what we should expect, along with equally meaningless good fortune. Such a universe would be neither evil nor good in intention. It would manifest no intentions of any kind. In a universe of blind physical forces and genetic replication, some people are going to get hurt, other people are going to get lucky, and you won't find any rhyme or reason in it, nor any justice. The universe we observe has precisely the properties we should expect if there is, at bottom, no design, no purpose, no evil, and no good, nothing but blind, pitiless indifference."

Is this the universe we live in? Does the Big Bang rule out the need for a God who loves and creates? If there is a God, can it be shown that he's merely a spectator, a nonessential observer of natural processes? This session will help group members grapple with the implications of this popular theory of the universe's origins.

1. From the time when you were in school, do you remember taking any course that taught things now considered outdated or even wrong? How do you think the professor would have reacted if you had known the future and could have predicted that his material would later be considered erroneous?

When the movie *Jurassic Park* was shown in Israel, it was condemned by some Orthodox rabbis because it accepted evolution and because it taught that dinosaurs lived a hundred million years ago—when, as is plainly stated at every Rosh Hashanah and every Jewish wedding ceremony, the Universe is less than 6,000 years old.

—Carl Sagan, *The Demon-Haunted World: Science As a Candle in the Dark*

2. What is your understanding of what the Big Bang theory is all about?

3. What aspects of the Big Bang theory are generally accepted by the scientific community? What aspects are disputed?

4. What part of the Big Bang theory makes believers in God nervous? Why do you think that is so?

5. Some have argued that the Big Bang theory actually supports belief in God, because it shows that the universe had a beginning. Do you agree? Why or why not?

STRAIGHT TALK

As Mysterious As a Religious Idea?

While the Big Bang theory has the endorsement of the vast majority of cosmologists, that doesn't mean the theory is easy to grasp. In fact, very few of the concepts that describe what supposedly occurred in the first few seconds after the Big Bang make any sense at all — at least in the way most of us think. Cosmologists readily admit that the laws of physics as we know them didn't apply in the early nanoseconds after the Big Bang.

Calling a theory "scientific" may still involve just as much mystery as does a concept related to theology (such as the Trinity or an omnipresent but undetectable God). Marilyn Vos Savant, listed in the *Guinness Book of World Records* as the person holding the highest IQ, wrote, "I think that if it had been a religion that first maintained the notion that all the matter in the entire universe had once been contained in an area smaller than the point of a pin, scientists probably would have laughed at the idea."

6. What is your reaction to the above statement by Ms. Vos Savant?

HEART OF THE MATTER

7. Why do you think some people who have very little scientific training feel the need to make strong statements in areas in which they are not well qualified to speak?

8. Why do you think people get so emotional when they engage in discussions about how the universe originated?

The Big Bang makes a thrilling scenario . . . of everything springing forth from that blinding flash, [which] bears a striking resonance with [the] words of Genesis 1:3: "And God said, 'Let there be light.'" Who could have guessed . . . a hundred years ago . . . a thousand years ago that a scientific picture would emerge with electromagnetic radiation as the starting point of creation! Astrophysicist Robert Jastrow thinks that the agnostic scientists should sit up and take notice, and even be a little worried.

—Owen Gingerich, *The World Treasury of Physics, Astronomy, and Mathematics*

9. Do you think the Big Bang theory disproves God or his role as creator? Why or why not?

10. If the universe has no creator and we are all just the dust of stars collected over billions of years, what impact does that have on how you view your life? What about how you view others?

11. If we are mere globs of star dust, an accidental accumulation of molecules forged in the furnace of trillions of suns, why should we take time to discuss questions like these? If we're creatures made by a loving God, artfully assembled in his image, why should we do so?

CHARTING YOUR JOURNEY

12. What statement(s) below best fits your thoughts right now? Explain your answer.

_____ I have read a lot about this subject and enjoy talking about it.

_____ I am conversant with these ideas and like to hear what others say.

_____ I tend to have strong opinions in this area, although I need to learn more before I speak too assuredly.

_____ I enjoy talking about this subject, but I
know very little.

_____ I felt really stupid during this discussion
because I am ignorant about scientific
theories regarding the universe's
beginning.

_____ Other: _____

_____

_____

Doesn't Evolution Contradict Genesis?

Who's the Real Monkey?

More than any other event in the twentieth century, the Scopes trial of 1925 showed the tension that exists in America between belief in the Bible and belief in science. When the defendant, John T. Scopes, was tried for teaching evolution, the trial turned into a circus pitting two well-known lawyers, William Jennings Bryan and Clarence Darrow, against each other. These two showmen turned a simple trial into a public forum on evolution, with Darrow showing the supposed narrow-mindedness of those who accept a literal interpretation of the book of Genesis as opposed to the factual, reasonable basis of modern science. Mocking the Genesis account, Darrow quipped, "[Adam and Eve] were allowed to stay there on one condition, and that is that they didn't eat of the tree of knowledge. That has been the condition of the Christian church from then until now. They haven't eaten as yet, as a rule they do not." He also maintained, "I am an agnostic; I do not pretend to know what many ignorant men are sure of."

Has time made the Genesis account any more acceptable to modern thinkers? If anything, evolutionary science has made even greater strides in disproving the notion of a meddling creator. As the 1995 National Association of Biology Teachers' statement says, "The diversity of life on earth is the outcome of

Geology shows that fossils are of different ages. Paleontology shows a fossil sequence, the list of species represented changes through time. Taxonomy shows biological relationships among species. Evolution is the explanation that threads it all together. Creationism is the practice of squeezing one's eyes shut and wailing "Does not!"

—posted on the Internet

evolution, an unsupervised, impersonal, unpredictable, and natural process of temporal descent with genetic modification that is affected by natural selection, change, historical contingencies, and changing environments." Though a few years later the statement was amended to take out the words *unsupervised* and *impersonal,* what's left is still a repudiation of any role God might have played in the process.

Which theory—evolution or special creation—best fits the facts? Which theory is open to change and modification based on added data? Which theory is emotionally held by those who know little about this topic but feel they're right anyway, and which theory is held by those committed to increasing their knowledge through research and investigation? Comparing the two camps, Stephen Jay Gould, author of *Dinosaur in a Haystack,* writes, "Our creationist detractors charge that evolution is an unproved and unprovable charade—a secular religion masquerading as science. They claim, above all, that evolution generates no predictions, never exposes itself to a test, and therefore stands as dogma rather than disprovable science. This claim is nonsense. We make and test risky predictions all the time; our success is not dogma, but a highly probable indication of evolution's basic truth." James Watson, winner of the Nobel Prize for his codiscovery of the structure of DNA, agrees: "Today, the theory of evolution is an accepted fact for everyone but a fundamentalist minority, whose objections are based not on reasoning but on doctrinaire adherence to religious principles."

So which is it—evolution or special creation? This session will not solve this hot issue, but it will help you explore the various opinions, and hopefully generate some light as well as heat.

I suspect that today if you asked people to justify their belief in God, the dominant reason would be scientific. Most people, I believe, think that you need a God to explain the existence of the world, and especially the existence of life. They are wrong, but our education system is such that many people don't know it.

—Richard Dawkins

Isn't it enough to see that a garden is beautiful without having to believe that there are fairies at the bottom of it too?

—Douglas Adams

1. Do you remember the first time you heard or read about the idea that humans evolved from lower forms of life? How did you react to that theory?

> Science has proof without any certainty. Creationists have certainty without any proof.
>
> —Ashley Montague

2. When you were growing up, were your parents and other spiritual leaders hostile to any aspects of human evolution? If so, what reasons did they give to support their opinions?

3. When you learned about human evolution in biology class (or another class), were you informed of any disputed areas of the theory? Cite any weaknesses or controversy you are aware of regarding the theory of evolution.

4. Do you consider yourself fairly knowledgeable in the area of life sciences (biology, anthropology, biochemistry, etc.)? How does that expertise (or lack of it) affect your ability to discuss the issue of evolution with clarity and conviction?

5. Do you think the account of Creation in Genesis 1 and 2 is incompatible with evolutionary theory? Why or why not?

6. What is at stake for a believer in the Bible if evolution is shown to be true? What is at stake for a believer in evolution if there is a God who created life?

STRAIGHT TALK

Just the Facts

Believers in God who are scientists object to evolution on the basis of evidence, not just on the basis of religious beliefs. Many scientists who are not theists also take issue with aspects of evolutionary theory. But when a prior commitment to exclude

God exists in the mind of a scientist, is it any wonder the evidence of God's handiwork goes unseen?

Materialists start with the presupposition "There is no God involved in the development of life on planet Earth (or elsewhere)" and then interpret the facts to fit that prior belief. Christians start with the presupposition "We would not be surprised to see evidence of design, because our Bible tells us a Designer made the universe." Both groups have their bias. Yet it still comes down to which model best accounts for the body of evidence we have.

Most scientists see the fossil record as showing transitions from simpler organisms to more complex ones. Yet the same data is interpreted differently by others. Phillip E. Johnson argues, "Of course God could have used a gradual, guided process to create. The problem with this idea isn't that God could not do it — the scientific problem is that the fossil evidence does not support evolutionary gradualism. You find the sudden appearance of all the major groups of living things without a detailed history of step-by-step development. If God did use a gradual process to create, he also chose not to leave the evidence of it lying around."

Because science is committed to finding an explanation that excludes God at all costs, it presses on to come up with some way to account for this suddenness. Even if science can't explain it, the one option not open is that of a creator. A Christian, however, would be more open to God's creative activity as a sufficient explanation — yet would remain receptive to new evidence that would modify that belief.

7. What evidence are you aware of that shows life is the product of intelligent design rather than random, naturalistic forces?

STRAIGHT TALK

A Question of Interpretation

Believers as well as critics agree that Genesis 1 and 2 have some poetic elements. For example, if God made sounds when he spoke, how was his voice heard without an atmosphere to carry the sound waves? Where did those sound waves originate (God doesn't have a mouth), and what language did he use? How could there have been what we normally mean by "evening" (the sun going down) and "morning" (the sun coming up) when the sun wasn't even created until the fourth day?

Bible-believing Christians differ on the meaning of some details of Genesis 1 and 2. One issue is the length of the days of creation; another is the age of the earth. All believers agree that God is the Creator and that we should expect to see evidence of his handiwork in creation. We must not reduce disagreements to a matter of whether to take the Bible literally or not. In every passage of Scripture, we must take the Bible for what it actually teaches, through whatever means of language the writer used (and the Bible contains many forms of literary devices). Surely, the author of Genesis knew that God isn't a physical being with a mouth and that there is no sunrise without a sun! This passage does teach that God literally created the universe and humankind, yet does so through undeniably poetic language requiring careful interpretation.

A seeker sometimes worries that he will be forced to accept ridiculous things in the name of accepting the Bible. ("If I become a Christian, will I have to believe that the Promised Land had milk and honey soaking into the ground everywhere, because the Bible says it was 'flowing with milk and honey'?") And believers are fearful that truth is being compromised because of a willingness to change Scripture to fit whatever theory is in vogue among atheistic scientists. Neither extreme is a problem if we keep coming back to the guiding question, What did the author really mean?

So handle Genesis carefully, neither making it say what it doesn't nor setting aside what it does!

8. What is your reaction to the claim that Genesis contains poetic elements? What is your reaction to the claim that it teaches we were created and didn't randomly evolve?

HEART OF THE MATTER

9. What emotions stir in you as you discuss the issue of evolution versus creation?

Genesis 1 and 2, however, tell us who without giving many answers about how.... The message of these two chapters is this: "Have you seen the sea? The sky? Sun, moon, and stars? Have you watched the birds and the fish? Have you observed the landscape, the vegetation, the animals, the insects, all the big things, and little things together? Have you marveled at the wonderful complexity of human beings, with all their powers and skills ...? Fantastic, isn't it? Well now, meet the one who is behind it all!" ... [Genesis] shows us the Creator rather than the creation and [teaches] us knowledge of God rather than physical science.

—J. I. Packer, cited in
The Case for Christianity

10. Do you think it's possible to be completely objective when discussing evolution versus creation? Why or why not?

11. What emotion do you suppose an atheistic scientist feels when encountering evidence of a creator? What emotion does a believer feel upon finding explanations for phenomena that don't require God's involvement?

CHARTING YOUR JOURNEY

12. On a scale from one to ten, place an X near the spot and phrase that best describes you. What reasons do you have for placing your X where you did?

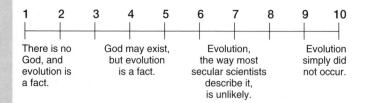

If the Bible Is True, Why Isn't It More Scientific?

An Omniscient Perspective?

Bible-believing people are fond of saying, "God never changes." This is meant to be comforting, to show that while circumstances change, God remains the same. Shouldn't the same be true about knowledge? Shouldn't God's knowledge never change? If the Almighty is behind the teaching in the Bible, shouldn't its content reflect a timeless knowledge of reality? Wouldn't we be a little suspicious if what is written in the Bible sounds a lot like the knowledge of the era in which it was written? Thomas Jefferson observed, "We discover [in the Gospels] a groundwork of vulgar ignorance, of things impossible, of superstition, fanaticism and fabrication." Isn't it in fact the case that the Bible does describe things from the pre-scientific point of view of its human authors?

If God is behind this text, why doesn't it sound more like the product of an infinitely knowledgeable deity who knows that stars aren't points of light—as they are described by an unlearned herdsman looking up at the sky while watching his sheep—but massive suns?

And what about all those miracles? Can thinking people believe that miracles really happened? Aren't we dealing with gullible people who didn't bother to look for natural explanations? As Robert Ingersoll, a critic of religion, begged in *The Gods*,

[The Bible is] a mass of fables and traditions, mere mythology.

—Mark Twain,
Mark Twain and the Bible

We know all about your moldy wonders and your stale miracles. We want a "this year's fact." We ask only one. Give us one fact for charity. Your miracles are too ancient. The witnesses have been dead for nearly two thousand years. Their reputation for "truth and veracity" in the neighborhood where they resided is wholly unknown to us. Give us a new miracle, and substantiate it by witnesses who still have the cheerful habit of living in this world. Do not send us to Jericho to hear the winding horns, nor put us in the fire with Shadrach, Meshech and Abednego. . . . It is worse than useless to show us fishes with money in their mouths, and call our attention to vast multitudes stuffing themselves with five crackers and two sardines. We demand a new miracle, and we demand it now. Let the church furnish at least one, or forever hold her peace.

Where in the Bible is the compelling truth that a modern-day scientist can look at and say, "This author clearly knew about the universe the way it really is, not the way the ancients thought it was"? Why does the Bible sound so unenlightened if its source is omniscient? This session will help you get answers to this tough question.

OPEN FOR DISCUSSION

1. Did your early spiritual teachers lead you to accept the Bible without question? What rationale were you offered for their certainty (or skepticism)?

2. What is your current level of confidence in the reliability of the Bible when it touches on matters of history or science?

3. If the Bible can be shown, through the science of archaeology, to be reliable in matters of history, would that affect your level of trust in it regarding other areas? Would you still trust the Bible if it taught things known to be historically or scientifically untrue?

STRAIGHT TALK

A Factual Comparison of The Book of Mormon and the Bible

One way to see the accuracy of the Bible is to open it alongside other so-called revelations from God. When we take a very popular contender in this area, the Book of Mormon, we find a drastic difference. Though the Bible isn't scientific, its archaeological accuracy compared with that of this other revered work stands out as strikingly superior.

The Book of Mormon	The Bible
Mythical creatures (satyrs and dragons) are mentioned as real, not figurative.	No such borrowing from Greek mythology.
Geographical anomalies: a river called Laman supposedly empties into the Red Sea (no such river exists or has existed); no correlation between known bodies of water in the New World and the Book of Mormon.	Bodies of water and other geological information mentioned correspond to what is known.
Not one city mentioned in the Book of Mormon (in the New World) has ever been discovered or excavated; there is no evidence for a massive civilization in the places and dates described.	Many cities in the Middle East have been identified as biblical sites and excavated; inscriptions linking those locations to the Bible are common.
Statement available from the Smithsonian Institution that says, "Smithsonian archaeologists see no direct connection between the archaeology of the New World and the subject matter of the book [of Mormon]."	Archaeologists regularly refer to biblical texts as they excavate in the Middle East.
The Book of Mormon contains many anachronisms betraying the writer's lack of accurate knowledge: steel, horses, cows, goats, chickens, silk, pigs, lions, candles, compasses, swords with hilts, spindles, bellows, trumpets, harps, scimitars, synagogues, and leprosy claimed to be in America before Columbus; people are called Christians in 73 B.C.; the book claims Jews spoke Egyptian from 600 B.C. to 91 B.C. (they spoke Hebrew, then Aramaic).	Bible events and artifacts consistent with era in which they're described, borne out by archaeology.

The Book of Mormon (cont.)	The Bible (cont.)
The Book of Mormon contains factual errors: Jesus supposedly born in Jerusalem (not Bethlehem); three days of darkness (rather than three hours); Malachi misquoted as saying, "Son of Righteousness" instead of "Sun of Righteousness" (a mistake possible by an English reader, but the Hebrew words do not sound alike); Native Americans used the phrase "Alpha and Omega" (the first and last letters of the Greek alphabet).	Such errors not found in the Bible; even if there are some disputed references, they allow for alternate explanations that do not imply error.
The Book of Mormon claims Native Americans were originally Jews who left the faith and became "a dark, and loathsome, and a filthy people" (1 Nephi 12:11); their skin coloring was a curse; African-Americans couldn't hold the priesthood until 1978 because of the belief that their dark skin proved they'd sinned before being born.	No such racial insults; God made sure that prejudicial attitudes were confronted and exposed (Acts 10:34–35).
The Book of Mormon, though purportedly translated letter for letter—not just word for word—by God (through the agency of Joseph Smith), contains curious phrases and descriptions that seem to indicate human, fallible authorship: a beheaded man gasps for breath, struggles, and then dies (Ether 15:30–31); phrases such as "all manner of—ites" (4 Nephi 17) and "cite your minds forward" (Alma 13:1) betray Joseph Smith's lack of knowledge of English.	Bible not dictated letter for letter; we don't have originals to compare, though very early copies ensure accuracy; the Book of Mormon original translation (1830 version) available to show thousands of changes since then (even though God gave Joseph Smith each letter individually, so why should even one letter be altered?).

4. What do you think of the these comparisons?

5. If archaeology ever did find an artifact that contradicted the Bible, what would that do to your faith? Explain.

6. Although the Bible is undeniably a prescientific book, do you think it teaches belief in outright errors? Why or why not?

STRAIGHT TALK

The Language of Observation

When a scientist says, "The sun will come up at 6:05 A.M.," we don't accuse him of being unscientific, even though any scientist knows the sun doesn't "come up" — the earth rotates. Similarly, the Bible usually describes phenomena from a human point of view, without the precision of a scientific journal. That should not surprise us, as the Bible came through common people and was designed to be understood by common people — not just by an elite group of scientists.

7. What is the difference between being imprecise and being in error? Do you think the Bible's descriptive language negates its reliability as a source for absolute truth? Explain.

HEART OF THE MATTER

8. What do you think about the enduring quality of the Bible, considering it's more than twenty centuries old and has been ruthlessly criticized by skeptics?

9. Why do you think some people seem to enjoy finding "contradictions" in the Bible?

10. When a parent talks to a young child, the parent often has to modify her mode of speaking so the child can understand. Do you think this analogy adequately explains why the Bible, though it claims to come from an omniscient God, is in common, everyday language—without scientific precision? Why or why not?

11. Check the statement(s) below that best reflects your opinion. What reasons do you have for choosing that statement(s)?

_____ There is no God, so it's no surprise that the Bible isn't scientific.

_____ The Bible's lack of precision is evidence that it isn't from God.

_____ The Bible's lack of precision means God doesn't get bogged down in details.

_____ The Bible is as accurate as it needs to be to convey its message.

_____ The Bible is more precise than people realize.

_____ The Bible is 100 percent accurate—our observations must be flawed.

_____ Other: _____

_____

_____

Won't Scientific Progress Make God Unnecessary?

The Dependable Voice of Reason

Around 475 B.C. the Greek Anaxagorus said, "Everything has a natural explanation. The moon is not a god but a great rock and the sun a hot rock." Surely, in his world of mythology and appeal to the many gods and goddesses, Anaxagorus was a lone voice of reason—and far ahead of his time. Without such voices, modern science would have never been born. If it weren't for the demand that phenomena be explained without reference to divinities (or Divinity), how could we ever have made any progress in science? Everyone would have just stood around and said, "The gods did it" or "God wills it." End of discussion. Back into our caves.

Precisely because we dared to believe that everything wasn't the whim of a god, we've found explanations that have led to greater discoveries and improvements in our quality of life. Did religion give us vaccines? In fact, the church resisted the germ theory of disease, attributing plagues to the wrath of God and calling on people to submit to his decrees. Even after rats and sewage were known to aid in the spread of disease, one town-planning group seriously

> To surrender to ignorance and call it God has always been premature, and it remains premature today.
>
> —Isaac Asimov

Formerly, when religion was strong and science weak, men mistook magic for medicine; now, when science is strong and religion weak, men mistake medicine for magic.

—Thomas Szasz

Think of how many religions attempt to validate themselves with prophecy. Think of how many people rely on these prophecies, however vague, however unfulfilled, to support or prop up their beliefs. Yet has there ever been a religion with the prophetic accuracy and reliability of science?

—Carl Sagan, *The Demon-Haunted World: Science As a Candle in the Dark*

proposed leaving the sewers open so God would have a means to send a plague should he so desire!

Why do we stubbornly hold on to the notion that there's a God behind it all? Can't people see that the dominos of ignorance are falling and that the final one to fall will be the belief in an invisible, undetectable God? As long as we can see it coming, why not accept it now? Admit the inevitable and stand tall in the freedom that there's no one out there watching. Throw off the shackles of superstition and live in the knowledge that we must make our destiny. Stop counting on God to come through—he's had enough time, and religion is exactly where it's always been, waiting in silence for the voice of a heavenly "Father" who's never going to show up, because we're orphans, not God's children.

Trust in the provable, logical, and testable world of science. Though not perfect, it's far superior to dogmatism. In the words of James Morrow, "Some people think it's profound to say that science doesn't have all the answers. They're wrong. Science does have all the answers—we just don't have all the science." Charles Darwin echoed that sentiment when he wrote in *The Ascent of Man,* "Ignorance more frequently begets confidence than does knowledge: it is those who know little, and not those who know much, who so positively assert that this or that problem will never be solved by science."

This session will help you wrestle with the question of why some say we might have to give up God if we want to move forward as a species, and it will help you see if it really is true that as science gets bigger, God gets smaller.

1. Describe a time when you had to drastically revise your view of God. What emotions came with that change?

2. It is undeniable that science has made great strides, especially in our generation. Why do you think people have such optimism about the possibility that science will answer all our questions and solve all our problems?

Science can destroy a religion by ignoring it as well as by disproving its tenets. No one ever demonstrated, so far as I am aware, the nonexistence of Zeus or Thor, but they have few followers now.

—Arthur C. Clarke, *Childhood's End*

3. What do you think of the following statement: "If we use God to explain what we cannot understand, God shrinks every time we learn something new"?

Is God on the Way Out?

Some people used to think lightning and thunder proved there was an angry god of the skies; naturalistic explanations have demystified those phenomena. Likewise, people once believed that Pele, the goddess of the volcano, needed to be appeased by a human sacrifice. Now we know there is no correlation between killing a human and the cessation of a volcanic eruption, nor is the goddess Pele required to explain plate subduction and magma flows, which create earthquakes and volcanoes.

Will the belief that the universe requires a designer be the next superstitious domino to fall, when science can account for what now requires a creator God to explain? As Chapman Cohen observed, "Gods are fragile things; they may be killed by a whiff of science or a dose of common sense." Will that also happen to the God of the Bible?

4. Will your god (if you believe in one) ever be "killed by a whiff of science or a dose of common sense"? Why or why not?

The more the fruits of knowledge become accessible to men, the more widespread is the decline of religious belief.

—Sigmund Freud

5. The "God of the gaps" fallacy says we use God to explain what science can't—we fill in the gaps of our knowledge with an appeal to the activity of God. Do you think that is the case with Christian theism? Explain.

6. Many areas of life (such as the act of falling in love) are not subject to empirical scientific testing or even to being improved though science. Despite this limitation of science, the notion persists that scientific knowledge will eventually do away with belief in God. Do you agree? Why or why not?

7. How has science strengthened your belief in God, if you are a believer? If you aren't a believer, what has science taught you that makes belief in God seem unreasonable?

HEART OF THE MATTER

8. What tough question(s) about some scientific issue still troubles you?

9. Read the following quote by Paul Davies, from his book *God and the New Physics*.

Every thing and every event in the physical universe must depend for its explanation on something outside itself. When a phenomenon is explained, it is explained in terms of something else. But if the phenomenon is all of existence and the entire physical universe then clearly there is nothing physical outside the universe (by definition) to explain it. So any explanation must be in terms of something non-physical and supernatural. That something is God. The universe is the way it is because God has chosen it to be that way. Science, which by definition deals only with the physical universe, might successfully explain one thing in terms of another, and that in terms of another and so on, but the totality of physical things demands an explanation from without.

Do you agree that something outside the universe is required to explain the universe sufficiently? Why or why not?

10. If you were to abandon all belief in God, what unsettling questions come to mind?

11. Can you imagine a discovery of science that would destroy your belief in God? Explain.

CHARTING YOUR JOURNEY

12. On a scale from one to ten, place an *X* near the spot and phrase that best describes your opinion. What reasons do you have for placing your *X* where you did?

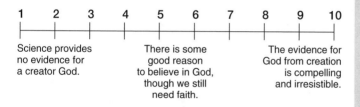

1   2   3   4   5   6   7   8   9   10

Science provides no evidence for a creator God.

There is some good reason to believe in God, though we still need faith.

The evidence for God from creation is compelling and irresistible.

Recommended Resources

Michael J. Behe, *Darwin's Black Box* (Touchstone, 1998).

Ken Boa and Larry Moody, *I'm Glad You Asked* (Chariot Victor, 1995).

Gregory Boyd and Edward Boyd, *Letters from a Skeptic* (Chariot Victor, 1994).

William Lane Craig, *Reasonable Faith* (Crossway, 1994).

William A. Dembski and Michael J. Behe, *Intelligent Design* (InterVarsity, 1999).

Michael Denton, *Evolution* (Adler and Adler, 1985).

C. Stephen Evans, *Why Believe?* (Eerdmans, 1996).

Phillip E. Johnson, *Darwin on Trial* (InterVarsity, 1993).

Cliffe Knechtle, *Give Me an Answer* (InterVarsity, 1986).

Andrew Knowles, *Finding Faith* (Lion, 1994).

Peter Kreeft and Ronald Tacelli, *Handbook of Christian Apologetics* (InterVarsity, 1994).

C. S. Lewis, *Mere Christianity* (HarperSanFransisco, 2001).

C. S. Lewis, *Miracles* (HarperSanFransisco, 2001).

Paul Little, *Know What You Believe* (Chariot Victor, 1987).

Paul Little, *Know Why You Believe* (InterVarsity, 2000).

J. P. Moreland, *Scaling the Secular City* (Baker, 1987).

Hugh Ross, *The Creator and the Cosmos* (NavPress, 2001).

Lee Strobel, *The Case for Christ* (Zondervan, 1998).

Lee Strobel, *The Case for Faith* (Zondervan, 2000).

WILLOW
Willow Creek Association

Willow Creek Association
Vision, Training, Resources for Prevailing Churches

This resource was created to serve you and to help you build a local church that prevails. It is just one of many ministry tools that are part of the Willow Creek Resources® line, published by the Willow Creek Association together with Zondervan.

The Willow Creek Association (WCA) was created in 1992 to serve a rapidly growing number of churches from across the denominational spectrum that are committed to helping unchurched people become fully devoted followers of Christ. Membership in the WCA now numbers over 10,000 Member Churches worldwide from more than ninety denominations.

The Willow Creek Association links like-minded Christian leaders with each other and with strategic vision, training, and resources in order to help them build prevailing churches designed to reach their redemptive potential. Here are some of the ways the WCA does that.

- **Prevailing Church Conference**—an annual two-and-a-half day event, held at Willow Creek Community Church in South Barrington, Illinois, to help pioneering church leaders raise up a volunteer core while discovering new and innovative ways to build prevailing churches that reach unchurched people.

- **Leadership Summit**—a once-a-year, two-and-a-half-day conference to envision and equip Christians with leadership gifts and responsibilities. Presented live at Willow Creek as well as via satellite broadcast to over sixty locations across North America, this event is designed to increase the leadership effectiveness of pastors, ministry staff, volunteer church leaders, and Christians in the marketplace.

- **Ministry-Specific Conferences**—throughout each year the WCA hosts a variety of conferences and training events—both at Willow Creek's main campus and offsite, across the U.S. and around the world—targeting church leaders in ministry-specific areas such as: evangelism, the arts, children, students, small groups, preaching and teaching, spiritual formation, spiritual gifts, raising up resources, etc.

- **Willow Creek Resources®**—to provide churches with trusted and field-tested ministry resources in such areas as leadership, evangelism, spiritual formation, spiritual gifts, small groups, stewardship, student ministry, children's ministry, the use of the arts—drama, media, contemporary music—and more. For additional information about Willow Creek Resources® call the Customer Service Center at 800-570-9812. Outside the U.S. call 847-765-0070.

- *WillowNet*—the WCA's Internet resource service, which provides access to hundreds of transcripts of Willow Creek messages, drama scripts, songs, videos, and multimedia tools. The system allows users to sort through these elements and download them for a fee. Visit us online at www.willowcreek.com.

- *WCA News*—a quarterly publication to inform you of the latest trends, resources, and information on WCA events from around the world.

- *Defining Moments*—a monthly audio journal for church leaders featuring Bill Hybels and other Christian leaders discussing probing issues to help you discover biblical principles and transferable strategies to maximize your church's redemptive potential.

- *The Exchange*—our online classified ads service to assist churches in recruiting key staff for ministry positions.

- **Member Benefits**—includes substantial discounts to WCA training events, a 20 percent discount on all Willow Creek Resources®, access to a Members-Only section on WillowNet, monthly communications, and more. Member Churches also receive special discounts and premier services through WCA's growing number of ministry partners—Select Service Providers.

For specific information about WCA membership, upcoming conferences, and other ministry services contact:

Willow Creek Association
P.O. Box 3188, Barrington, IL 60011-3188
Phone: 847-570-9812
Fax: 847-765-5046
www.willowcreek.com

Tough Questions

Garry Poole and Judson Poling

"The profound insights and candor captured in these guides will sharpen your mind, soften your heart, and inspire you and the members of your group to find vital answers together."

—Bill Hybels

This second edition of Tough Questions, designed for use in any small group setting, is ideal for use in seeker small groups. Based on more than five years of field-tested feedback, extensive revisions make this best-selling series easier to use and more appealing than ever for both participants and group leaders.

Softcover

How Does Anyone Know God Exists? ISBN 0-310-24502-8

What Difference Does Jesus Make? ISBN 0-310-24503-6

How Reliable Is the Bible? ISBN 0-310-24504-4

How Could God Allow Suffering and Evil? ISBN 0-310-24505-2

Don't All Religions Lead to God? ISBN 0-310-24506-0

Do Science and the Bible Conflict? ISBN 0-310-24507-9

Why Become a Christian? ISBN 0-310-24508-7

Leader's Guide ISBN 0-310-24509-5

Pick up a copy today at your favorite bookstore!

ZONDERVAN™

GRAND RAPIDS, MICHIGAN 49530 USA

WWW.ZONDERVAN.COM

WILLOW

Willow Creek Resources

THE COMPLETE BOOK OF QUESTIONS

Garry Poole

Everyone has a story to tell or an opinion to share. *The Complete Book of Questions* helps you get the conversational ball rolling. Created especially for seeker small groups, these questions can jumpstart any conversation. They invite people to open up about themselves and divulge their thoughts, and provide the spark for stimulating discussions. This generous compilation of questions can be used in just about any context to launch great conversations.

Questions cover ten thematic categories, from light and easy questions such as "What room in your house best reflects your personality?" to deeper, more spiritual questions such as, "If God decided to visit the planet right now, what do you think he would do?" *The Complete Book of Questions* is a resource that can help small group leaders draw participants out and couples, friends, and families get to know one another better.

Softcover: ISBN 0-310-24420-X

Pick up a copy at your favorite local bookstore today!

WILLOW
Willow Creek Resources

ZONDERVAN™

GRAND RAPIDS, MICHIGAN 49530 USA

WWW.ZONDERVAN.COM

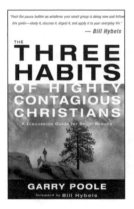

Reality Check Series

by Mark Ashton

Winning at Life
Learn the secrets
Jesus taught his disci-
ples about winning at
life through the
stories he told.

Saddle Stitch

ISBN: 0-310-24525-7

Jesus' Greatest Moments
Uncover the facts and
meaning of the provo-
cative events of the
final week of Jesus'
life.

Saddle Stitch

ISBN: 0-310-24528-1

Leadership Jesus Style
Learn the leadership
principles taught and
lived by Jesus.

Saddle Stitch

ISBN: 0-310-24526-5

Hot Issues
Find out how Jesus
addressed the chal-
lenges of racism,
feminism, sexuality,
materialism, poverty,
and intolerance.

Saddle Stitch

ISBN: 0-310-24523-0

When Tragedy Strikes
Discover Jesus' per-
spective on the prob-
lem of suffering and
evil in the world.

Saddle Stitch

ISBN: 0-310-24524-9

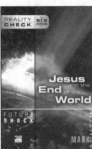

Future Shock
Uncover Jesus'
perspective on the
mysteries of the future
as revealed in the
Bible.

Saddle Stitch

ISBN: 0-310-24527-3

Sudden Impact
Discover the life-
changing power of
Jesus as he interacted
with his contempor-
aries.

Saddle Stitch

ISBN: 0-310-24522-2

Clear Evidence
Weigh the arguments
for and against the
Jesus of the Bible.

Saddle Stitch

ISBN: 0-310-24746-2

Pick up a copy today at your favorite bookstore!

ZONDERVAN™
GRAND RAPIDS, MICHIGAN 49530 USA
WWW.ZONDERVAN.COM

WILLOW
Willow Creek Resources

THE CASE FOR CHRIST

Lee Strobel

Is Jesus really the divine Son of God? What reason is there to believe that he is?

In this bestseller, investigative reporter Lee Strobel examines the claims of Christ. Written in the style of a blockbuster investigative report, *The Case for Christ* puts the toughest questions about Christ to experts in the fields of science, psychology, law, medicine, biblical studies, and more.

The result is a powerful narrative that will convince seekers and believers alike of the proven reality of Jesus Christ.

"Lee Strobel asks the questions a tough-minded skeptic would ask. Every inquirer should have it."

—Phillip E. Johnson, law professor,
University of California at Berkeley

Hardcover	ISBN 0-310-22646-5
Softcover	ISBN 0-310-20930-7
Evangelism Pack	ISBN 0-310-22605-8
Mass Market 6-pack	ISBN 0-310-22627-9
Abridged Audio Pages® Cassette	ISBN 0-310-21960-4
Unabridged Audio Pages® Cassette	ISBN 0-310-24825-6
Unabridged Audio Pages® CD	ISBN 0-310-24779-9
Student Edition	ISBN 0-310-23484-0
Student Edition 6-Pack with Leader's Guide	ISBN 0-310-24851-5

Pick up a copy at your favorite local bookstore today!

WILLOW
Willow Creek Resources

ZONDERVAN™

GRAND RAPIDS, MICHIGAN 49530 USA
WWW.ZONDERVAN.COM

THE CASE FOR FAITH

Lee Strobel

Was God telling the truth when he said, "You will seek me and find me when you seek me with all your heart"?

In his bestseller *The Case for Christ*, the legally trained investigative reporter Lee Strobel examined the claims of Christ, reaching the hard-won yet satisfying verdict that Jesus is God's unique Son.

But despite the compelling historical evidence that Strobel presented, many grapple with doubts or serious concerns about faith in God. As in a court of law, they want to shout, "Objection!" They say, "If God is love, then what about all of the suffering that festers in our world?" Or, 'If Jesus is the door to heaven, then what about the millions who have never heard of him?"

In *The Case for Faith*, Strobel turns his tenacious investigative skills to the most persistent emotional objections to belief, the eight "heart" barriers to faith. *The Case for Faith* is for those who may be feeling attracted to Jesus but who are faced with formidable intellectual barriers standing squarely in their path. For Christians, it will deepen their convictions and give them fresh confidence in discussing Christianity with even their most skeptical friends.

Hardcover	ISBN 0-310-22015-7
Softcover	ISBN 0-310-23469-7
Evangelism Pack	ISBN 0-310-23508-1
Mass Market-6 pack	ISBN 0-310-23509-X
Abridged Audio Pages® Cassette	ISBN 0-310-23475-1
Unabridged Audio Pages® Cassette	ISBN 0-310-24825-6
Unabridged Audio Pages® CD	ISBN 0-310-24787-X
Student Edition	ISBN 0-310-24188-X
Student Edition 6-Pack (with Leader's Guide)	ISBN 0-310-24922-8